the CRAZY world of SCHOOL

Cartoons by Bill Stott

EXLEY
NEW YORK • WATFORD, UK

CU00601572

Other books in this series:
The Crazy World of Aerobics (Bill Stott)
The Crazy World of Cats (Bill Stott)
The Crazy World of Cricket (Bill Stott)
The Crazy World of Gardening (Bill Stott)
The Crazy World of the Greens (Barry Knowles)
The Crazy World of Golf (Mike Scott)
The Crazy World of the Handyman (Roland Fiddy)
The Crazy World of Hospitals (Bill Stott)
The Crazy World of Housework (Bill Stott)
The Crazy World of Learning to Drive (Bill Stott)
The Crazy World of Marriage (Bill Stott)
The Crazy World of Photography (Bill Stott)
The Crazy World of Rugby (Bill Stott)
The Crazy World of Sailing (Peter Rigby)
The Crazy World of Sex (David Pye)
The Crazy World of Soccer (Bill Stott)

Published simultaneously in 1995 by Exley Publications Ltd. in Great
Britain, and Exley Giftbooks in the USA.

Copyright © Bill Stott 1991

12 11 10 9 8 7 6 5 4 3 2 1

ISBN 1-85015-016-8

Printed and bound by Grafo S.A., Bilbao, Spain.

Exley Publications Ltd, 16 Chalk Hill, Watford, Herts WD1 4BN,
United Kingdom.
Exley Giftbooks, 232 Madison Avenue, Suite 1206,
NY 10016, USA.

"My mother says I'm her little angel, were you ever a little angel, Mr. Sidebottom?"

*"I wonder what you have to do wrong to grow up
like Mr. Trimblett?"*

"I'm having parental trauma. They'd like me to go into medicine. I want to be a bimbo."

"Come on Doris, you have to see the funny side ..."

"Yes, we find her difficult to control, too …"

"He tells me to fasten my tie properly – and look at the state of him!"

"Jason lacks concentration Mr. Fittock ... MR. FITTOCK!"

"*The foreign legion regret that they have no vacancies just now.*"

"We always knew putting Mr. Warburton with 3B was a gamble ..."

"So do I, Gary, so do I."

"Hold it Miss Bainbridge – I think the ass wants to wee."

"If he's got a first class degree, I don't think I want one."

"*Idle, insolent, shiftless? Did I write that? Well, well …*"

"*The trouble with educational jokes is that you might end up working for them ...*"

"Oh, and you've got Melainie Bainbridge out here exercising her right as a sun worshipper not to go to assembly."

"It's amazing! I told him my homework would be late because a volcano erupted under our house ... and he believed me!"

"While Kirsty may have torched your lab – may I remind you that her father is head of the P.T.A.?"

"Mr. Hardisty's letting 3B get to him ..."

"'_Course_ teachers lie – read that!"

"Wouldn't it be great if, just once, nurse discovered somebody with a really horrible disease?"

"Sex education with 3B is quite an experience, eh Miss Wellbeloved?"

"The new teacher's got a confidence problem."

"But Sharon – bright red zits with big yellow heads right on
the end of your nose are all part of life's rich tapestry."

"Why did I opt to do art? Simple. They wouldn't have me in music, drama, chemistry, French, biology, technology or history."

"Miss! Miss! Melody Hargreaves has thrown up on Henry
the hamster!"

"I've bought an executive-style briefcase, had my hair re-vamped, grown a fashionable moustache – and the little beasts still throw things at me ..."

"I want to be sure you love me for my mind as well as
my body ..."

"'Morning Debbie – which one of your fan-club did your homework this week?"

"*I'm looking for the chewing gum you made me throw away last Monday …*"

"Please sir, Catriona Everard is telling tales again!"

"*Correction Mrs. Harmsworth, Terence doesn't 'play' truant –
he's dead serious about it!*"

"*Rules or no rules Flanagan, I've a good mind to box your ears ...*"

"And if NASA have no vacancies – what then?"

"Mr. Fittock's nostrils are even hairier than my grandad's!"

"Sir? How do you draw cleavages?"

"It was just bad luck sir. <u>Anybody</u> could make a bad smell during assembly!"

"The lad's a trier – he started that coffee table in the first year."

"I'm afraid the lunch hour art club will have to disband – Louise McFadden is offering life poses to anybody who'll do her homework."

"So far, Headmaster, we've had 397 calls claiming responsibility ..."

"*I suppose one of the hidden bonuses of sports day is seeing the Head in his tracksuit.*"

"*I'm just not the swimming type sir. Sometimes I throw up
in the bath!*"

"*Geoffrey Wilson won't tell me what French kissing is, Miss....
What's French kissing Miss?*"

"You certainly know where you stand with this new Head …"

"Threatening me with your father is useless Tomkinson. I have it on good authority that like you, he is a wimp."

"… and that's our Mr. Whiteside. In theory, a brilliant
chemistry teacher. In practice …"

"Dad sent a note Miss ..."

"Just another reason why I hate gym."

"Leave him alone. Only an idiot tries to keep 3B in detention on the last day of term ..."

"*I'm warning you 3B. I have a B.A., an M.A., and a Ph.D. and I will find out who made that awful smell!*"

"Well, the Head will need hospitalizing, but it is a new record."

"We'd like her on our team – her game's fairly average, but she swears better than John McEnroe!"

"Cute! She said you were cute!"

"Aw come on – my dad told me about it – you go behind the bike sheds and it all happens!"

"What's this secret project I've been hearing about?"

"It must be fantastic to be in the last year – imagine being able to go to the toilet without asking!"

"What we have here, Headmistress, is the logical extension of the 'my dad can beat your dad up' syndrome ..."

"You ask me why I get such a lot of time off? There go three good reasons."

"Somewhere along the line we're going wrong – according to Fiona Pratt tadpoles come from frogs bonking."

"*I have no doubt that you would like to be a mercenary when you leave, Clinton, but it's going to help if you spell it correctly on the application form ...*"

"We all get pimples from time to time Joanne – now take your
head out of the desk, there's a good girl …"

"*Cheating? No sir. I just happened to sit behind someone with the answers written on the back of his white sweater sir.*"

"Why am I in detention? Because when Mrs. Lovejoy asked if there were any questions, I asked her why she always asked if there were any questions when there never were ..."

"Once many years ago, I held a class spellbound ..."

"So it's true about Mr. Leapwell leaving teaching?"

"He's a hero in our class. Miss Parkinson accused him of acting like Rambo."

"This apple is not just a gift, Miss. The fact is – I love you."

Books in the "Crazy World" series
($4.99 £2.99 paperback)

The Crazy World of Aerobics (Bill Stott)
The Crazy World of Cats (Bill Stott)
The Crazy World of Cricket (Bill Stott)
The Crazy World of Gardening (Bill Stott)
The Crazy World of Golf (Mike Scott)
The Crazy World of The Handyman (Roland Fiddy)
The Crazy World of Hospitals (Bill Stott)
The Crazy World of Housework (Bill Stott)
The Crazy World of Learning to Drive (Bill Stott)
The Crazy World of Love (Roland Fiddy)
The Crazy World of Marriage (Bill Stott)
The Crazy World of The Office (Bill Stott)
The Crazy World of Photography (Bill Stott)
The Crazy World of Rugby (Bill Stott)
The Crazy World of Sailing (Peter Rigby)
The Crazy World of Sex (David Pye)
The Crazy World of Soccer (Bill Stott)

Books in the "The World's Greatest" series
($4.99 £2.99 paperback)

The World's Greatest Cat Cartoons
The World's Greatest Computer Cartoons
The World's Greatest Dad Cartoons
The World's Greatest Golf Cartoons
The World's Greatest Marriage Cartoons
The World's Greatest Sex Cartoons

Books in the "Mini Joke Book" series
($6.99 £3.99 hardback)

These attractive 64 page mini joke books are illustrated
throughout by Bill Stott.

A Binge of Diet Jokes
A Bouquet of Wedding Jokes
A Feast of After Dinner Jokes
A Knockout of Sports Jokes
A Portfolio of Business Jokes
A Round of Golf Jokes
A Romp of Naughty Jokes
A Spread of Over-40s Jokes
A Tankful of Motoring Jokes
A Triumph of Over-50s Jokes
A Megabyte of Computer Jokes

Books in the "Victim's Guide" series
($4.99 £2.99 paperback)

Award winning cartoonist Roland Fiddy sees the funny side
to life's phobias, nightmares and catastrophes.

The Victim's Guide to Air Travel
The Victim's Guide to the Baby
The Victim's Guide to the Boss
The Victim's Guide to the Christmas
The Victim's Guide to the Dentist
The Victim's Guide to the Doctor
The Victim's Guide to Middle Age